Tractatus Ph

CW00447533

Praise for *Tractatus Philosophico-Poeticus*

'Signe Gjessing's highly original reconfiguration of Wittgenstein's *Tractatus* unfolds at once logically and lyrically on the trembling cusp where philosophy and poetry intersect. Her witty, haunting propositions shimmer between the profound and the puzzling, and beautifully enact Wallace Stevens's assertion that "Life's nonsense pierces us with strange relation".'
    – Mark Ford

'Fuelled both by logic and intuition, luxuriance and clarity, ecstasy and precision, this long poem unfurls, fractal-like, to amass moments of confounding, generative insight and beauty.'
    – Ralf Webb

'Signe Gjessing is a wild voice in new Danish poetry, always closely connected to the symbolic tradition and cosmos.'
    – Naja Marie Aidt

'Signe Gjessing is Wittgenstein plus rapture. In her reimagining of the *Tractatus*, poetry is a verb; an action to be found in transgressions and transitions. Like a silken butterfly emerging from its cocoon.'
    – *Information*

Tractatus Philosophico-Poeticus
by Signe Gjessing

Translated by Denise Newman

Lolli Editions

Foreword

The poem *Tractatus Philosophico-Poeticus* is
a rewriting of Ludwig Wittgenstein's philosoph-
ical treatise *Tractatus Logico-Philosophicus*.
I have adapted Wittgenstein's ingenious sys-
tem, which was an attempt to create a lan-
guage of logic, with sentences subdivided
by mathematics: proposition 1.01 comments
on proposition 1. Proposition 1.011 comments
on the comment to 1. Proposition 1.1 is the
following thought, dictated by 1. Proposition 2
is something completely new, but follows
logically from 1. Wittgenstein wanted to unite
the disciplines of logic and philosophy in his
Tractatus. In my poem, I want to unite philoso-
phy and poetry and create propositions that
self-create into poetry, while still possessing
the logical consistency of philosophy. Like
Wittgenstein, I am concerned with the *limit*,
which is what determines his *Tractatus*. But
ecstasy is also my basis – something new
in relation to Wittgenstein, who recognised
ecstasy as a possibility outside his work,
although within it, he wanted to reproduce
the limits of what can be said.

My intent for the individual lines in the poem
is that they may say what cannot be said.
They are based on universal dimensions in
order to confront what comes after *everything*,
and which ought not to be possible to say.
The unsayable is thereby identified with the
transcendent and the limit of meaning
becomes that of the quantity. If the poem is
considered an accumulation of logical units,

a proposition that follows the concept of *the world* should be unsayable since the world ascribes the meaning: *everything that exists.* As such, the poem is a modification of the universal – as though the sayable were an incapacity of the unsayable. If, as Wittgenstein proposed, we view the sentence as a 'logical scaffolding' (*Tractatus* 3.42), then, by virtue of the poem's logical structure, it already stands outside the concept of *everything*.

The poem works with ecstasy as the premise of the world. The world's possibility is ascribed an ontological precedence to the world's existence, because it is the starting point that the world transcends through its creation. The world's character of possibility implies that the many worlds' logical possibilities are binding. The world as phenomenon is viewed through Set Theory and the impossibility of certain quantities that are not themselves part of a quantity. The poem is composed around a thought-up world, ecstatic presence, and final annihilation.

Wittgenstein borrowed his title from Baruch de Spinoza's treatise *Tractatus Theologico-Politicus*.

S.G.

1 The world looks out,
then arises, in beauty.

1.01 *Here* is the world.

1.011 Reality slips
right through
here.

1.0111 Possibilities discover
reality's shortcut:
The world arises.

1.1 The world is
everything
that is evident.

1.11 Being expects the world, that is all.

1.12 Being promises the possible worlds too much: The world.

1.121 Roses may be a bit too delicate when compared to the stars.

1.1211 Rosestars?
The stars need
to sleep on it first.

1.2 A world leads
to unrest.

1.3 The world must
be seen as an
approximation.

1.31 It goes against the uni-
verse to universalise
itself too hard,
during the summer
it universalises
itself so very loosely.

1.311 A universe may seem
like chance when it
loses concentration.

1.312 Not much silk
is needed in a new
universalisation.

1.4 **The sensation of being in the world may be supplemented by a bit of being, if you like.**

2   Here, being passes by
         the most obvious.

2.1   Over there is
         only being.

2.2   No, no, being disturbs
         nothing at all.

2.3   Being belongs
         to no one.

2.4   Being is mitigating
         circumstances:
         Nothing.
         And yet.

2.41 The universe alludes to silence when it 'is'.

2.5 Being can anticipate when something wants to exist because it goes around saying it wants to be immortal.

3 The world is
imported.

3.01 The world is a good
alternative to certainty.

3.011 The world has been
allowed to sit and
watch from one
side of the balance.
The world is not
supposed to shift the
balance, it should
just watch.

3.02 Is it completely
intentional that
the universe
has not led roads
to the stars?

3.03 The universe always
shows up at the last
minute, right before
universality gives up.

3.031 And always with some
kind of new scent.

3.1 The world is accentu-
ated by the drops
as an example.
– *Which ecstasies?*
– *The world,* e.g.

3.2   Glimpses of the world
        are the beyond that
        stop while the going
        is good.

3.3   The world is
        formalities.

3.31   If we don't uphold
        formalities – such
        as thinking about
        the light – then we
        are beyond.

3.311   As for the world, it is
        done with forgetting.

3.4   Great demands are
put on the world's
transcendence:
The world has
to disappear from
there not *here*.

3.41   The world has its
beginning to thank
for its elusiveness.

3.411   The world's creation
is followed up with *very*
different initiatives.

3.5   The world is a mild
        regret for actions.

3.51   The actions are
        beyond.

3.511   The answer to the
        beyond must read:
        Yes, but also there.

3.5111 Transcendence:
        Holding a space for
        the world in infinitely
        many places.

3.6   The world exports
a shampoo based
on stars and longing.

3.61   Distance has lost its
grip on the cosmic:
Meanwhile the
migrating world
sends stars
out every day.

3.7   The beyond follows
us and holds up the
world like a bridal veil:
Avant-garde.

3.71   The world's light-
        ness is not the same
        as its ecstasy.

3.711   The world weighs
        less than my
        problems.

3.7111 But a universe and
        universality use
        the same size idea.

3.8   The world's race is
        an extra loop.

3.81   After the universe,
        everything is fresh.

3.82   The length repeats
        the universe for
        those slow-witted
        mountains:
        Travelling.

3.9   Of and with the
        universe I exist.

3.91   The universe always
        has swimsuit stars on.
        Just in case.

3.92   The universe in fact
        helps the everything
        with extra water
        and roses.

3.10   We call out using the
         universe's son-name.

3.11   The universe joins
         the silk team.

3.12   The world is a collec-
         tive name for the
         world-inducers who
         wander off.

3.121   The world is only
         the curious among
         the world-inducers.

3.1211   The world's visits
           out and about
           are symbolic.

3.12111   The world's visits out
           and about drag on
           so that the roses take off.

3.121111   Worlds are roses in
           a children's edition.

3.12112   The worlds find their
           natural bearings
           after being all the
           way out.

4   Causation's
          neighbour is free.

4.01   The necessary
          must take a short
          trip beyond, and
          everything must be
          forgotten.

4.011   The roses were just
          about to pack up
          and leave everything
          when the universe
          fell in love with
          the law of causation.

4.02   Free worldery.

4.1 To the will: But the world already has causation...?

4.2 The world is hypostasised freedom.

5   Yes, we're in the world in question, yes, we are in it.

5.1   The world signals something a bit particular.

5.2   The world is a special type that one knows well from other situations where love is involved.

5.21   The world can in
       no way see itself
       in such a situation:
       Weak ecstasy.

5.22   With the world,
       love ceases having
       to create.

5.221 Not even a world
       is a matter of course
       when love creates.

5.2211 Love creates small
       medallions of
       universality.

5.3   The universe is
       as lonely as a gift idea:
       For inspiration.

5.31   Because the universe
       gives darkness private
       lessons, there's
       only one universe:
       Private lessons on
       the unpredictability
       of love.

5.4   Worlds seal off
       like a tree crown.
       Here lives my blood,
       the silkworm.

5.41 If you let the universes slip into each other, they all slip out via the small paths, which are divine.

5.411 The worlds have lots of things in common, but these things are just God.

5.412 The world is the only explanation for the height-differences of the universes.

5.5   I don't have a steady
        universe, but I have
        a steady rose.

5.51   The world often shifts
        wonder.

5.511   The world leaves
        everything to the roses
        which leave everything
        to chance.

5.6   There are vanishingly
        few worlds.

6 The world is no. 1.

6.01 The world is, if not
an exception, then an
exceptional occurrence
of inexperienced
creation.

6.1 Even if you subtract
all the silk, the world is
still the most cosmic.

6.11   It's a good thing that
        we have silk to tell fairy
        tales to materiality,
        but do they have
        to be so long?

6.111   The stars pack the
        silk on top and
        the ladies just below.

6.12   Has the world
        completely given up
        on transcending
        without silk?

6.2   The world is the good objective that the cherry trees of the possible worlds turn to – it's so hard to collect enough.

6.21   As soon as they're collected, someone gets an idea about what else they should be used for.

6.22   The world believes its possibility deserves to be seen.

7   Everything gives the
            impression of a world.

7.01   That which exists
            reads it like this.

7.011   *I* am more uncertain
            about how everything
            should be understood.

7.1   The world contradicts
            the ubiquitous:
            Everything is 'here',
            not everywhere.

7.2   The fall is the next
            'world'.

7.21   The everything is the
        worlds' security.

7.22   The world passes.

7.3   The world can in fact
        easily arise, exist and
        disappear.

7.31   It's the silk that is
        tricky to carry and
        often gets dirty,
        not the world.

7.4   *Everything* disappears
        only when it has
        completely lost sight
        of the world.

7.5   The world is something
       everything
       ought to.

7.51   The world is caught
       in the idea of
       an infinite number
       of worlds.

7.511 But the world is a bit
       of everything... a bit
       of the flowers, a bit
       of the water...

7.5111 Water has received
       a list of what it should
       wash over, and the
       universe is at the top.

7.512 More about the world:
It prefers flowers
before it perishes and
water *afterwards*.

7.5121 Wasn't there...
wasn't there a world
enclosed?

7.6 The needs of the world
are few, even though
it has so much.

7.7 The world was created
to lure distance, but
has the opposite effect.

7.71   Worlds have that all-
or-nothing mentality,
which is completely,
completely un-
necessary and just
so unfortunate.

7.8   The everything is one
of the few bright spots
in my life.

Biographies

Signe Gjessing (b. 1992) is a Danish poet. She graduated from the Danish Academy of Creative Writing, *Forfatterskolen*, in 2014. She has published several collections of poetry and a novella, and is the recipient of numerous awards and prizes, including the prestigious Bodil & Jørgen Munch Christensen Prize for emerging writers. *Tractatus Philosophico-Poeticus* is her first work to appear in English.

Denise Newman is a poet and translator based in San Francisco. She is the author of five poetry collections and the translator of *Azorno* and *The Painted Room* by Inger Christensen, and by Naja Marie Aidt, *Baboon*, winner of the PEN Translation Award, and *When Death Takes Something From You Give It Back: Carl's Book*, a semi-finalist for the National Book Award.

Tractatus Philosophico-Poeticus is No. 8
in the series New Scandinavian Literature

Graphic design by Ard – Chuard & Nørregaard

Printed and bound in the United Kingdom
by Healey's

Lolli Editions gratefully acknowledges
the support of the Danish Arts Foundation
and the Fondation Jan Michalski. This
translation was made possible through
their generous support.

Danish Arts
Foundation

FONDATION
JAN MICHALSKI
POUR
L'ECRITURE
ET LA
LITTERATURE

A CIP catalogue record for this book is available
from the British Library

ISBN 978-1-9196092-8-7

Lolli Editions
111 Charterhouse Street
London EC1M 6AW
United Kingdom
www.lollieditions.com